Thank you for your purchase.

We hope you enjoy colouring these patterns as much as we do!

Now claim your free bonus at

www.colorwithkim.com/amazon

Download 20 free adult colouring patterns - perfect for printing and colouring at home, as many times as you like!

Plus exclusive news, updates and more coloring goodies at colorwithkim.com

COLOR
with KIM
ADULT COLORING PATTERNS BY
KIM JONES

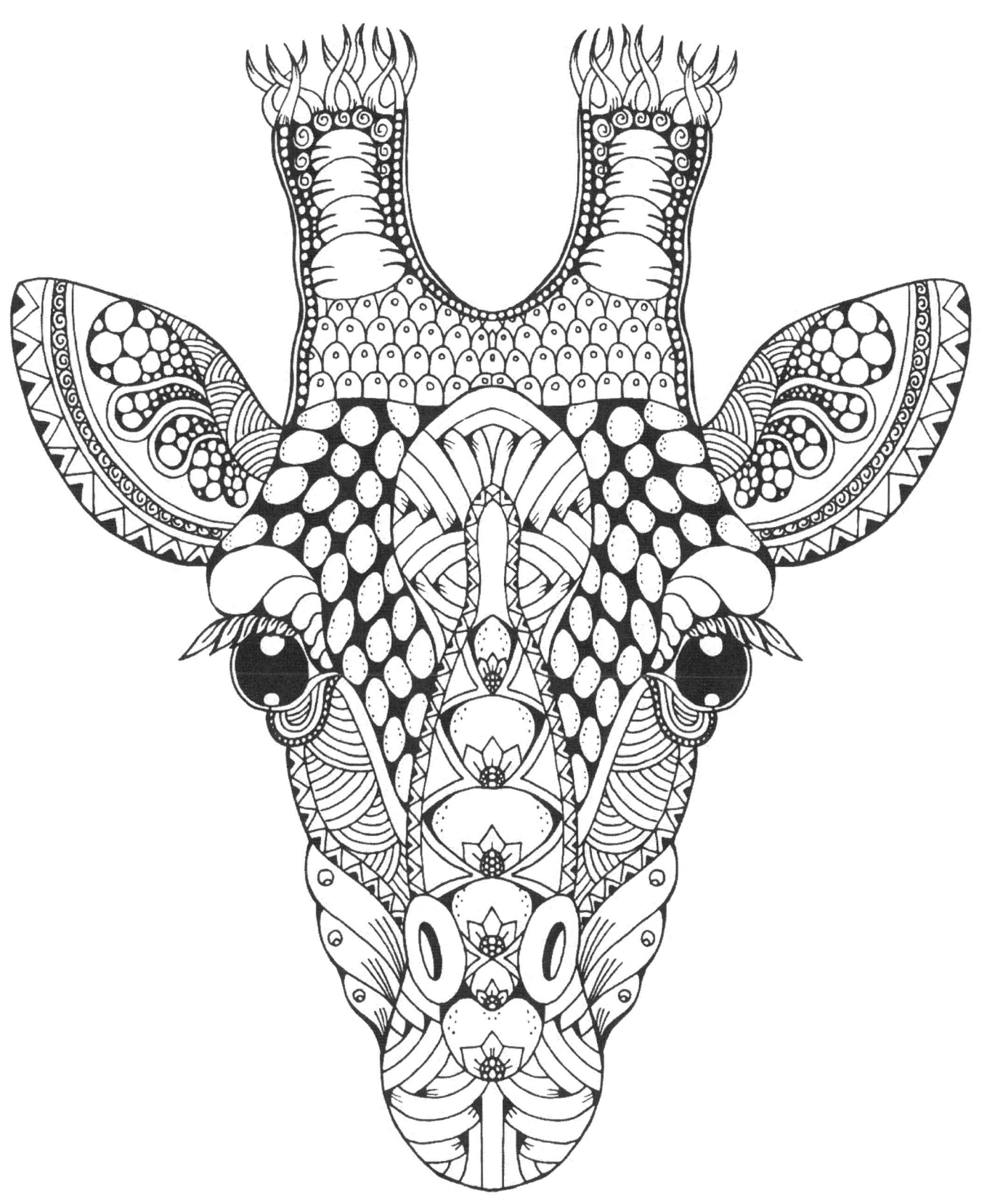

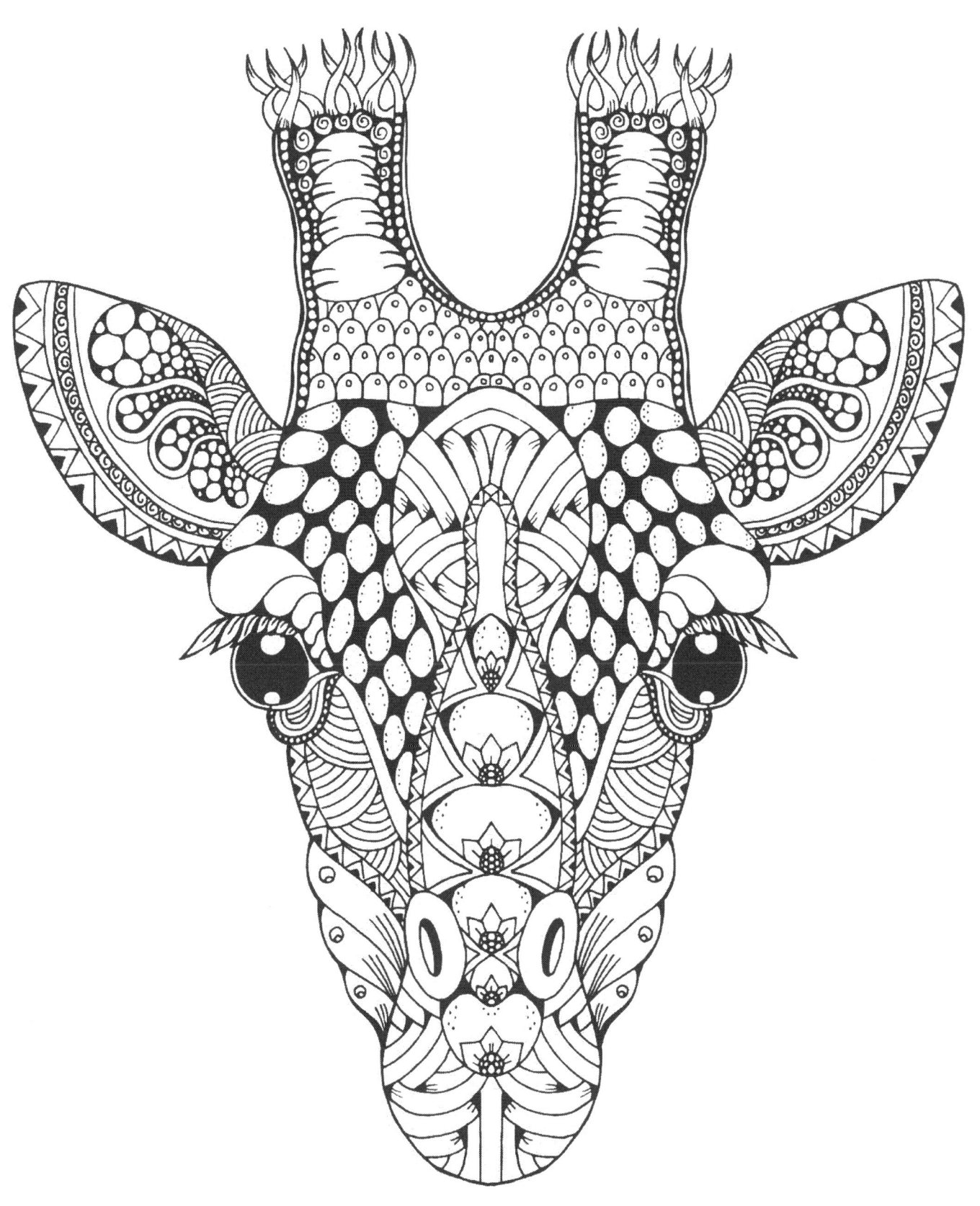

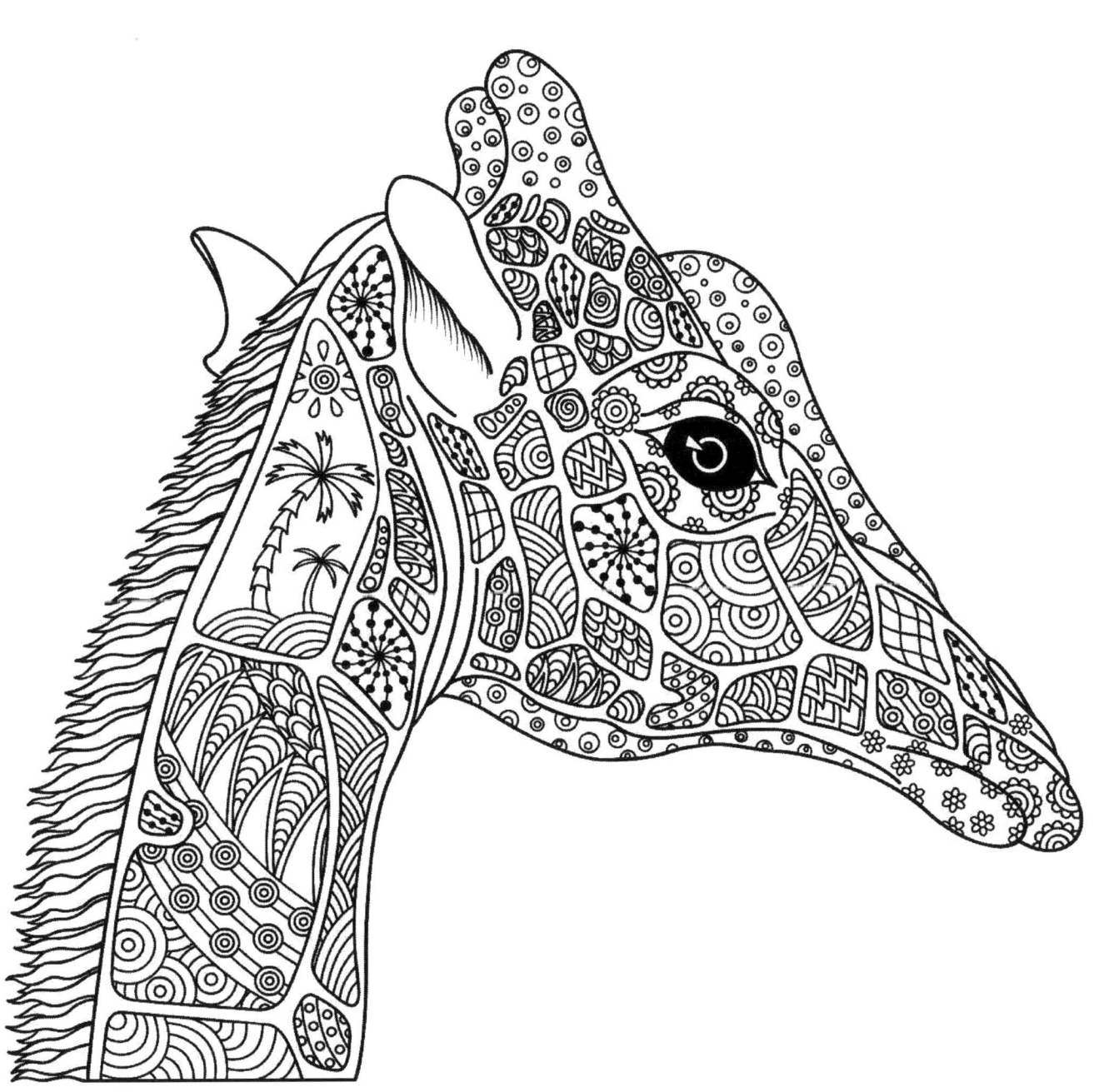

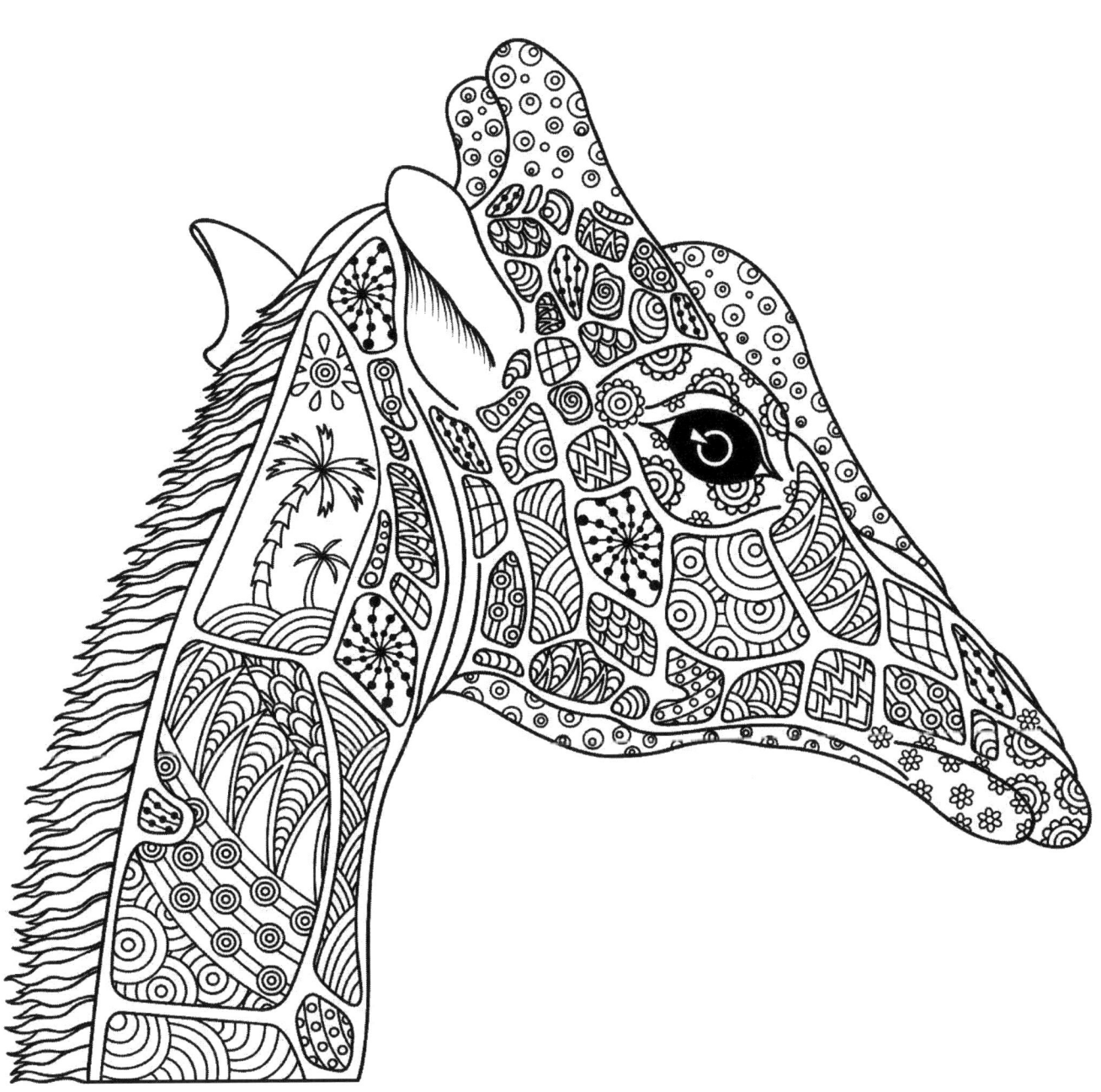

Printed in Great Britain
by Amazon